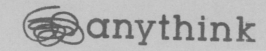

OASIS OF THE SEAS

BY QUINN M. ARNOLD

CREATIVE EDUCATION • CREATIVE PAPERBACKS

Published by Creative Education and Creative Paperbacks
P.O. Box 227, Mankato, Minnesota 56002
Creative Education and Creative Paperbacks are imprints
of The Creative Company
www.thecreativecompany.us

Design by The Design Lab
Production by Chelsey Luther
Art direction by Rita Marshall
Printed in the United States of America

Photographs by Alamy (All Canada Photos, Simon Brooke-Webb,
Fernando/Stockimo, Jim Lundgren, Phil Rees, Perry van Munster,
ZUMA Press, Inc.), Getty Images (Miami Herald), Newscom
(PHOTOPQR/OUEST FRANCE)

Library of Congress Cataloging-in-Publication Data
Arnold, Quinn M.
Oasis of the seas / by Quinn M. Arnold.
p. cm. — (Now that's big!)
Includes bibliographical references and index.
Summary: A high-interest introduction to the size, speed, and pur-
pose of one of the world's largest passenger ships, including a brief
history and what the future holds for the Oasis of the Seas.

ISBN 978-1-60818-715-7 (hardcover)
ISBN 978-1-62832-311-5 (pbk)
ISBN 978-1-5660-751-3 (eBook)
1. Oasis of the Seas (Cruise ship)— Juvenile literature. 2. Cruise
ships—Juvenile literature.

VM381.A75 2016
387.2/432—dc23   2015045210

CCSS: RI.1.1, 2, 3, 4, 5, 6, 7; RI.2.1, 2, 4, 5, 6, 7, 10; RF.1.1, 3, 4;
RF.2.3, 4

First Edition HC 9 8 7 6 5 4 3 2 1
First Edition PBK 9 8 7 6 5 4 3 2 1

TABLE OF CONTENTS

What is bigger than the Eiffel Tower but floats? In 2009, *Oasis of the Seas* became the first cruise ship to carry more than 6,000 passengers. It is still one of the biggest passenger ships in the world.

Rooms that face the park have balconies to enjoy the view.

The *Oasis* has 18 decks. It is as wide as a soccer field and almost four football fields long. In the middle of the ship is a park! Trees and thousands of plants grow there.

Allure of the Seas *is just two inches (5.1 cm) longer than* Oasis.

The ship was the first of Royal Caribbean International's *Oasis* class. The second *Oasis* class ship was finished in 2010. It is called *Allure of the Seas*.

2010

Oasis ships are built in a dry dock, where water can be drained or let in.

Six engines power the ship's three propellers. Each engine is the size of a bus! The propellers are each 20 feet (6.1 m) tall. The *Oasis* has a top speed of 26 miles (41.8 km) per hour. It uses a lot of fuel.

engine   school bus

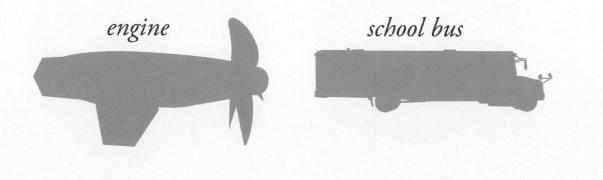

People watch as the ship stops in the Bahamas, Mexico, and other places.

Many people enjoy cruising on the *Oasis*. It can carry up to 6,296 passengers and 2,394 crew. The ship sails through the Caribbean Sea. It stops at several cities.

Some cities had to build special docks to fit the enormous Oasis.

Most trips last three to
eight days. Then the
ship docks for one day.
It lets people off and
loads fresh supplies.
New passengers come
on the ship.

The ship's AquaTheater seats up to 750 people for each show.

People on the *Oasis* stay busy. There are places to listen to music and watch movies. Passengers can play mini golf, rock climb, or swim. They can even go zip-lining!

All Oasis ships have a helicopter landing pad for emergency use.

Royal Caribbean continued to make *Oasis* class ships. The even grander *Harmony of the Seas* came out in 2016. Bigger ships are sure to follow!

2016

HOW BIG

OASIS OF THE SEAS
◄······ *1,186.5 ft (362 m)* ······►

EMPIRE STATE BUILDING
◄······ *1,454 ft (443 m)* ······►

TITANIC
◄······ *883 ft (269 m)* ······►

FIRST-GRADER
3.6 ft (1.1 m)

SEMITRAILER TRUCK
◀····*70 ft (21.3 m)*····▶

BLUE WHALE
◀····*100 ft (30.5 m)*····▶

SPACE SHUTTLE
◀····*122 ft (37.2 m)*····▶

GLOSSARY

class—*a group of similarly made ships*

crew—*the people who work on a ship*

decks—*the levels of a ship*

docks—*anchors or ties up in a place where people can get on and off*

engines—*machines that use fuel to create movement*

propellers—*parts powered by engines that help a ship go forward*

READ MORE

Stewart, Melissa. *Titanic*.
Washington, D.C.: National Geographic, 2012.

Zimmermann, Karl. *Ocean Liners: Crossing and Cruising the Seven Seas*.
Honesdale, Penn.: Boyds Mills Press, 2008.

WEBSITES

Ships and Boats Coloring Pages
http://www.supercoloring.com/coloring-pages/transport/ships-and-boats
Select from a variety of ships and boats to print off and color.

Water Bottle Boats
http://www.pbs.org/parents/crafts-for-kids/water-bottle-boats-video/
Build your own boat to float or race from recycled materials.

Note: Every effort has been made to ensure that the websites listed above are suitable for children, that they have educational value, and that they contain no inappropriate material. However, because of the nature of the Internet, it is impossible to guarantee that these sites will remain active indefinitely or that their contents will not be altered.

23

INDEX